Lift Every Voice and Sing

A PICTORIAL TRIBUTE TO

THE NEGRO NATIONAL ANTHEM

by JAMES WELDON JOHNSON

JUMP AT THE SUN

HYPERION BOOKS FOR CHILDREN

NEW YORK

Photo credits are found on page 32.

Book design by Sylvia Frezzolini Severance
Printed in Hong Kong.
First Edition
10 9 8 7 6 5 4 3 2 1

This book is set in Venetian 14/20.

Library of Congress Cataloging-in-Publication Data
Johnson, James Weldon, 1871–1938
Lift every voice and sing: a pictorial tribute to the Negro national anthem
/by James Weldon Johnson.
p.   cm.
Summary: Black-and-white photographs accompany this version
of the song that has come to be considered the African American
national anthem.
ISBN 0-7868-0626-5 (trade)—ISBN 0-7868-2542-1 (library)
1. Songs, English—United States—Texas.
[1. Afro-American—Songs and music. 2. Songs.] I. Title
PZ8.3.J6334 Li 2000
782.42164'089'96073—dc21
00-21227

An Anthem for All

"Lift Every Voice and Sing" is by many reverently called "The Negro National Anthem." The history of this memorable song and the two brothers who brought it into being make it an anthem for all time, and for all people.

James Weldon Johnson (1871–1938) and John Rosamond Johnson (1873–1954) were born in Jacksonville, Florida. Their father, James Johnson, who worked as the headwaiter in the prestigious St. James Hotel, exemplified the value of hard work, a virtue he passed on to both of his sons.

Their mother, Helen Dillett Johnson, was a teacher in the public school system of Jacksonville. She was also an accomplished musician who gave piano lessons to her younger son, John Rosamond. James Weldon, it seems, was more interested in writing than in music.

James Weldon, a very scholarly student, graduated from Jacksonville's Stanton High School when he was sixteen. After completing studies at Atlanta University in Atlanta, Georgia, he returned to Jacksonville, where at the age of twenty-three he was appointed principal of Stanton High School.

As time went by, James Weldon and John Rosamond each followed his own career path. James Weldon studied law, and became the first African American to be admitted to the Florida Bar. But for this creative gentleman, the practice of law was not a satisfying occupation. He soon turned his attention to the study of literature and creative writing. After intensive work with Brander Matthew, a professor on the faculty at Columbia University, James Weldon wrote his first novel, the tragically poignant *The Autobiography of an Ex-Coloured Man*, published in 1912.

John Rosamond Johnson graduated from The New England Conservatory of Music in 1897. He then journeyed to New York, where he found success writing musical scores for vaudeville shows and Broadway plays, including a version of *Beauty and the Beast*.

In 1900, when James Weldon and John Rosamond were together in Jacksonville, they composed "Lift Every Voice and Sing." The brothers were asked to write a piece for the Stanton High School chorus to sing in a special celebration of Abraham Lincoln's birthday. After they composed the song, five hundred young voices gave it life by performing it for the Abraham Lincoln birthday celebration.

As years passed, the song's popularity grew. And, nearly twenty years after it was originally composed, the NAACP proclaimed the thoughtful and reverential work as "The Negro National Anthem."

Over time the song has become one of the most honored compositions ever created. Perhaps this is so because the song's lyrics are all-inclusive. They embody a special and personal message for most listeners:

Faith: ". . . full of the faith that the dark past has taught us . . ."

Belief: "Let us march on, till victory is won . . ."

The Power of Prayer: ". . . shadowed beneath Thy hand,

may we forever stand . . ."

As a very young child in Harlem I sensed the emotion with which each adult sang the words to "Lift Every Voice and Sing." Then, when I learned the words in "elocution" class, I began to understand the adult emotions that "Lift Every Voice and Sing" calls to mind.

This very special book marks the centennial of the year the song was composed. Here you will find stunning photographs that chronicle the life and times of African American people from the era of enslavement to present day. These unforgettable images are sure to evoke emotions that have now become an indelible part of my life whenever the first chord is struck and all present begin to "lift every voice and sing."

—Henrietta M. Smith

Ms. Smith is Professor Emerita in the School of Library and Information Science at the University of South Florida. She is also a member of the Coretta Scott King Task Force.

Lift every voice and sing
            Till earth and heaven ring,
                        Ring with the harmonies of Liberty;

Let our rejoicing rise
    High as the listening skies,
Let it resound loud as the rolling sea.

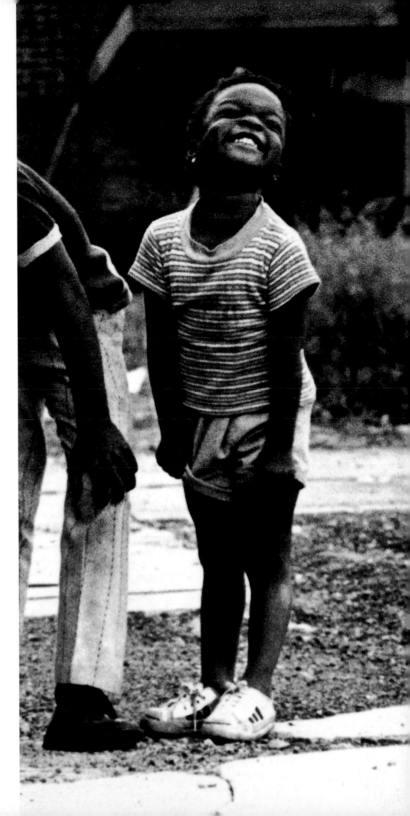

Sing a song full of the faith
    that the dark past has taught us,
Sing a song full of the hope
    that the present has brought us;

Facing the rising sun
of our new day begun,
Let us march on till
victory is won.

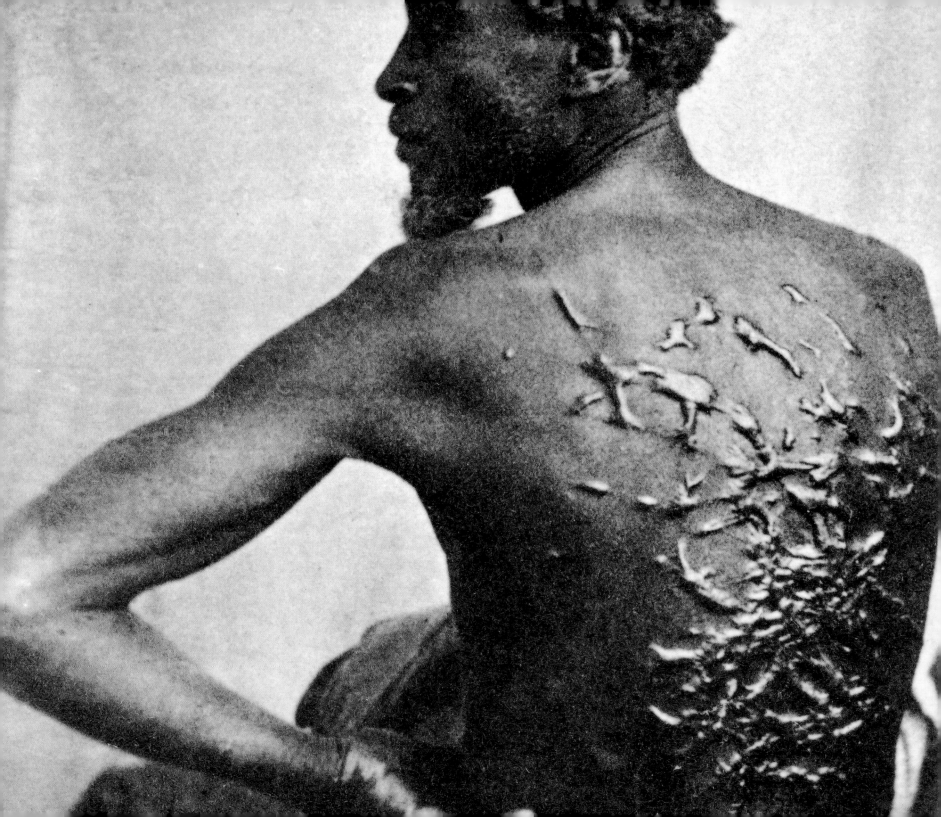

Stony the road we trod,

　　Bitter the chastening rod,

Felt in the days when

　　hope unborn had died;

Yet with a steady beat,
    Have not our weary feet
Come to the place for
    which our fathers sighed?

We have come over a way that
with tears has been watered,
We have come, treading our path through
the blood of the slaughtered,

Out from the gloomy past,
Till now we stand at last
Where the white gleam
of our bright star is cast.

God of our weary years,

God of our silent tears,

Thou who has brought us

thus far on the way;

Thou who has by Thy might
Led us into the light,
Keep us forever in the path,
we pray.

Lest our feet stray from the places,
    Our God, where we met Thee;
Lest, our hearts drunk with the wine
    of the world, we forget Thee;

Shadowed beneath Thy hand,
May we forever stand.
True to our God,
True to our native land.

Lift Every Voice and Sing

Maestoso ben sostenuto

JAMES WELDON JOHNSON, J. ROSAMOND JOHNSON

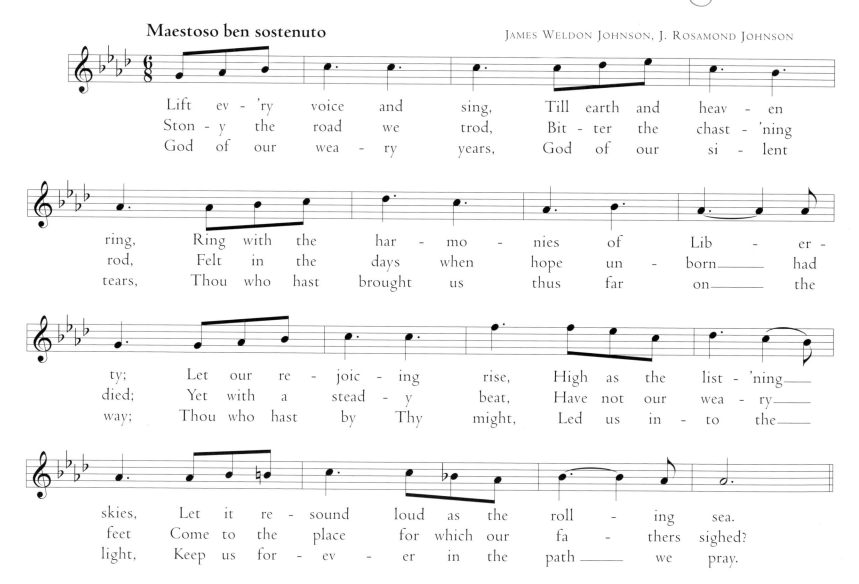

Lift ev - 'ry voice and sing, Till earth and heav - en
Ston - y the road we trod, Bit - ter the chast - 'ning
God of our wea - ry years, God of our si - lent

ring, Ring with the har - mo - nies of Lib - er -
rod, Felt in the days when hope un - born had
tears, Thou who hast brought us thus far on the

ty; Let our re - joic - ing rise, High as the list - 'ning
died; Yet with a stead - y beat, Have not our wea - ry
way; Thou who hast by Thy might, Led us in - to the

skies, Let it re - sound loud as the roll - ing sea.
feet Come to the place for which our fa - thers sighed?
light, Keep us for - ev - er in the path we pray.

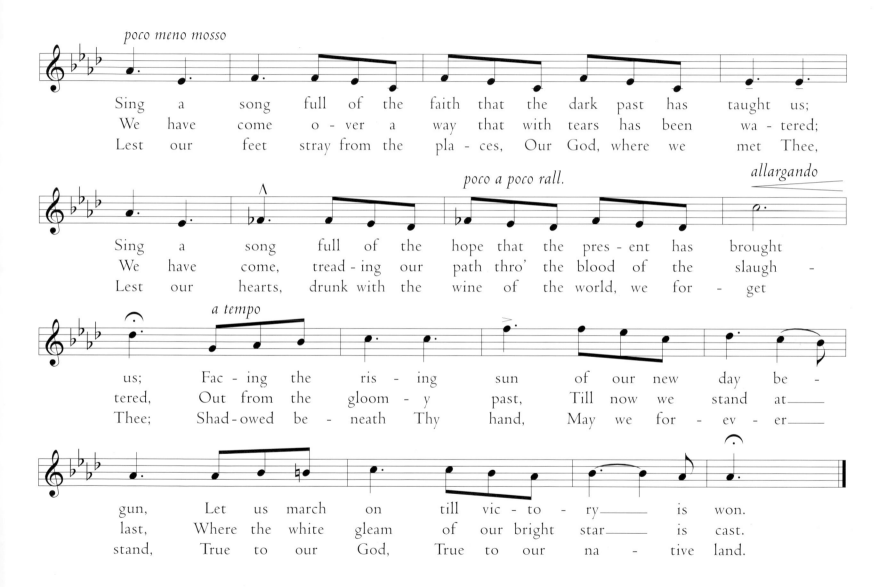

PHOTO CREDITS